UNDERCOVER UBER

An Investigative Report

DOUGLAS EDWIN CASIMIRI

© 2017 Douglas Edwin Casimiri
All rights reserved.
No part of this book may be reproduced, stored in a retrieval system, or transmitted by any means without the written permission of the author.

Published by Douglas Casimiri   Web: positivepastlife.com
Email: doug@positivepastlife.com
ISBN: 1545459487
ISBN: 9781545459485

Because of the dynamic nature of the Internet, any web address or links contained in this book may have changed since publication and may no longer be valid.
The views expressed in this work are solely those of the author and do not necessarily reflect the views of the publisher. The publisher hereby disclaims any responsibility for them.

TABLE OF CONTENTS

Introduction	vii
About the Book	ix
History of Uber	1
Founding	2
Funding	3
Surge Pricing	4
Rating Score	5
Opposition	6
Uber Protecting Consumers	7
Uber Driver Compensation	8
Driver Safety	13
Kidnapped	17
Change of Clothes	18
Mall Shopping	19
Gay Party Invitation	21
Passed Out	23
Throw-Up Tag Team	24
Grey Goose Fun	25
Private Screening	27
Bad Part of Town	28

Till Death Do Us Part	30
Hot-Headed Latino	33
Driver from India	35
Gay Driver	37
Unfriendly Driver	39
Reptilian Driver	41
Transvestite Driver	43
Tattoo Girl	44
Tire Change	46
Angry Husband	47
Wrong People	49
Possible Terrorist	51
Apartment Girl	53
Lost Bra	55
Three Broken Phones	56
Lunch, Anyone?	57
Transgender	59
Possible Drug Run	60
Urine in Car	61
Wine Opener	62
Surrounded in the Hood	64
Mass Murderer	65
Saved by Uber Driver	66
Two Girls	68
Pregnant Woman	69
Lottery Ticket	70
No Religion Here	72
Threesome, Anyone?	74
The Prepper	76
Let's Strip	79
Country Singers	80

Day of Shopping	81
Death of Father	82
A Woman's Fantasy	84
Sex Anywhere	86
Better Hide	87
Lost by GPS	89
Bad Online Date	91
Babysitter	93
Radio Management	95
Orgy, Anyone?	96
Thrown Out of Car	98
Clothing Optional	99
Run for Your Life	100
Not Ready	101
Bad Car Odor	102
Guns	104
Senior Encounter	105
Jealous Boyfriend	107
Female Drivers	109
Gentlemen's Club	111
Pool Party	113
Dumpster Diving	115
Glazed Doughnut	116
The Floater	118
Last Sex Wish	120
Working-Girl Chauffeur	122
Who Are Uber Drivers?	123
Final Note on Money and Uber	125
Press Release	126
About the Author	129

INTRODUCTION

I first heard about Uber from a friend of mine. He shared some of his stories of situations that he had been involved in while driving for Uber. He knew I was a writer and suggested I should become an underground driver (so to speak) to investigate the monetary per-hour claims Uber states their drivers make and to write about the situations drivers find themselves in every day.

So I decided to do just that. I filled in the application. I have to give Uber credit—Uber did an extensive criminal background check followed by DOT driving history. Uber also demands a minimum standard for your vehicle. The standards were much higher than those of most cabs I see driving passengers around today. You also send in your picture, which is then attached to your app. This way your passengers see a picture of you and know it's you when you arrive to pick them up. This is a tremendous safety feature that you don't receive with a regular cab. The fact that Uber knows who the driver is and Uber knows who the rider is goes a long way in preventing any undesirable situations.

The training is a short how-to video. I never spoke to anyone during the application process—it's all done online. If you have any questions or concerns, again, it's all done online. There is virtually no human contact through the whole process.

How Uber works is that when a passenger calls for a ride, the app sends the signal to the nearest Uber driver in the area. The driver receives a beeping circle on his or her phone. The driver then has about ten seconds to touch the circle if he or she wants to accept the ride; if the driver doesn't accept the ride, it will go to the next-nearest driver.

Once the ride is accepted by the driver, the GPS directs the driver to the pickup location. The passenger enters the address of the drop-off location into his or her phone, which pops up on the driver's phone, and again the GPS takes over and directs the driver to the passenger's desired location. When the driver has arrived at the designated location, the driver then slides the red banner at the bottom of the phone to end the trip. At that time, the cost to the passenger comes up, and the driver gets to rate the passenger from one to five, and the passenger gets to rate the driver. No money changes hands. The total is automatically charged to the passenger's credit/debit card. The technology is incredible.

Instead of the cab companies trying to stop Uber, they should come up with their own system to compete. If we were to tear down every new idea that comes along because the old system failed to compete, we would never have gotten out of the Stone Age.

ABOUT THE BOOK

The stories contained in this book were gathered over a period of about one year. All drivers shared their stories in complete confidentiality, and the participants were all assured I would not use any names (which I don't know anyway) or locations. This provides protection for all.

A lot of the stories came from riders that were Uber drivers or used to be Uber drivers. My own stories are mixed in with the rest of the stories. When I picked up fellow Uber drivers (they would always tell you), I would ask them to tell me about their craziest story involving a rider they had picked up. Every driver has at least one.

Remember, these stories were taken from thousands of riders. Ninety-nine percent of the riders are great and never pose a problem. But there is this very small group of riders that made the accounts in this book come to life.

This book contains graphic description of sexual situations, violence, and language. I tried the capture the intensity of emotion that the drivers must have felt during some of these accounts.

Warning: Reader Beware!

HISTORY OF UBER

Uber is an American transportation company headquartered in San Francisco, California. It develops, markets, and operates the Uber mobile app. This app allows the passenger to request a trip, which is then routed to the closest Uber driver. As of May 28, 2015, the service is available in fifty-eight countries and three hundred cities worldwide.

Uber was founded as UberCab by Travis Kalanick and Garret Camp in 2009, and the app was released the following June. It raised $49 million in venture funds by the start of 2011. Beginning in 2012, Uber expanded internationally. Uber continuously raised additional funding, reaching $2.8 billion in total funding by the start of 2015.

Of course, with any great ideas, the old guard protested against Uber, alleging that its use of unlicensed drivers (last time I checked, Uber drivers have licenses) was unsafe and illegal. You want to see unsafe? Call for a cab in any major city, and see what picks you up.

It was estimated that Uber would generate $10 billion in revenue by the end of 2015. This must be very upsetting to the old guard, who want to control and regulate everything. As usual, there is a part of our society that always has something against great ideas and the free-enterprise spirit.

FOUNDING

The idea for Uber came to Travis Kalanick when he was trying to find a cab to attend a 2008 LeWeb conference in Paris, France, but could not find one. Kalanick has stated this was the inspiration for Uber.

Uber was founded as UberCab by Travis Kalanick and Garrett Camp in 2009. The service was launched in San Francisco in June of 2010. Ryan Graves was appointed as CEO. Graves later stepped down from that role to become VP of operations and was replaced by Kalanick. Uber's mobile app for iPhone and Android phones was launched in San Francisco in 2010.

FUNDING

The company received venture funding in late 2010 from First Round Capital and a group of super angels in Silicon Valley that included Chris Sacca. In early 2011, Uber raised more than $11.5 million in series A funding led by Benchmark Capital. In late 2011, Uber raised an additional $32 million in funding from several investors including Goldman Sachs, Menlo Ventures, and Bezos Expeditions, bringing its total funding to $49.5 million.

Google Ventures invested $258 million in 2013.

By August 2014, the company had raised $1.5 billion.

In May of 2015, Uber revealed plans to raise between $1.5 and $2 billion in new funding, raising the value of the company to $50 billion or higher.

Uber is expanding internationally. Paris was the first city outside the United States to adopt the service, with many more countries coming online every day.

SURGE PRICING

Uber uses an automated algorithm to increase prices to surge levels. This allows Uber to respond to rapidly changing market conditions. Customers receive notice when making an Uber request that prices have been increased. At peak times, the prices can be four times the normal price.

RATING SCORE

Users of the app may rate the drivers; in turn, the drivers may rate the users. A low rating might diminish the availability of the service for the user.

OPPOSITION

As you would expect, Uber has numerous legal challenges from government, taxi unions, and so forth. They all want to bring down one of the greatest ideas ever created in the transportation industry. These attacks are to protect the poorly run organizations, such as cab companies, public transportation and so on, thus allowing them to carry on business as usual, never having to compete with a better product, price, and service.

The mistruths that governments and taxi unions put out there about the safety of Uber are appalling. They talk about lack of insurance. Uber has far superior insurance than most other companies. When a rider gets into an Uber car, there is a waybill that accompanies that rider with complete insurance information. They talk about the quality of the vehicles. Have you even seen a lot of the cabs lately? A 1999 Crown Victoria seems to be the cab of choice. They talk about the unsafe drivers. Do yourself a favor, and take a cab in a big city. Don't tell me those drivers have had extensive background checks. A lot of the countries these cab drivers come from have no ability to do a criminal background check or a DOT check. There is definitely a safety issue when you use a cab.

UBER PROTECTING CONSUMERS

Another thing you don't hear a lot about is the substantial reduction in alcohol-related accidents after Uber comes to town.

A new report by Uber and Mothers against Drunk Driving shows that the Uber is not just convenient and affordable—it is a lifesaver. People use Uber as a designated driver instead of trying to drive home by themselves. The report states when people have more options, they make better choices. In a survey of 807 individuals conducted by Berenson Strategy Group, 88 percent of the respondents agreed with the statement that Uber has made it easier for them to avoid driving home when they have had too much to drink, and 78 percent said Uber made it less likely that their friends would drive after drinking. The survey results are supported by other data.

So much for opponents of Uber, who will now have a more difficult time claiming that Uber puts the public at risk.

PS: Have you ever tried to get a cab after a night on the town? The wait time is ridiculous, and the cost is prohibitive. Uber solves all these consumer issues.

UBER DRIVER COMPENSATION

This is an area I have some concern over. I have spent substantial time as a driver, and I have asked other drivers to document their time and costs related to driving for Uber.

Recently Uber reduced the compensation to the drivers by almost 20 percent. I know some drivers who quit because of it. This also may be the reason Uber is advertising for drivers—it seems that on every station you turn on, you hear Uber commercials. If you listen to the commercials Uber is running, they seem to be targeting young people who may be new to the workforce, and how much the drivers truly make is not that important to Uber.

Uber doesn't care how many drivers they have in the same area. They make their money off of everybody, but a lot of the time there just isn't enough business for everyone.

Based on the new rates for drivers, you have to be constantly busy picking up riders to even achieve minimum wage after you subtract your costs.

Here are some examples of what drivers are making. To be fair, I am sure there are some drivers (the top 2 percent) who are doing very well and manage to be around for a lot of the surcharges. Even the surcharges are coming into question, as a new app from Uber allows the rider to be contacted after the surge period to avoid the surcharges. What I am talking about is the average driver and what they can expect to really earn driving for Uber.

Of course the city you work in, the size, and the demographics will also determine your earning power.

A lot of the pickups and drop-offs are at the minimum charge of $4. The driver may have to drive three to four miles to pick the rider up and then drive another two to four miles and drop the rider off.

Let's break down the minimum charge by Uber. First, Uber receives an automatic $1 from every rider. We have to subtract the $1 from the $4, which leaves a balance of $3. Now Uber takes 20 percent of the $3, which equals $0.60. The amount the driver receives is $2.40 gross income, minus the driver's expenses.

I have tracked and found that the average fuel cost per hour for me is $3. Of course, this fuel cost will vary depending on fuel economy of the vehicle.

Total time for this pickup, drop-off, and the return to wherever you position yourself is about twenty minutes. The total distance traveled may be eight to ten miles.

The driver would have used about half a gallon of gas, which cost $1.50 at the time of this writing, plus the wear and tear on the vehicle.

The net profit to the driver is $2.40 gross profit – $1.50 = $0.90. As you can see from this equation, there is no way you can make money. The most riders you could reasonably service is about four riders per hour at this minimum charge.

A lot of the time, riders will ask you to take them shopping or other activities that involve some wait time. Uber pays the drivers $0.13 per minute of wait time. I am going to give you an example of what that really means to the driver. You take someone grocery shopping. That person is charged an initial minimum charge of

$4. You wait thirty minutes. Thirty minutes x $0.13 per minute = $4.20 in wait time. You take the client back home and help unload the groceries. The total charge will be around $10. Uber really discourages riders from tipping, which also really hurts the driver. Altogether the driver has spent at least forty-five minutes to one hour with this rider. The profit would be $10 gross charge – $1 for Uber = $9.

Uber receives 20 percent of the $9, which equals $1.80.
$9 – $1.80 = $7.20 for the driver.
$7.20 – $1.50 for gas = $5.70 net profit for the driver.

Let's look at longer-distance runs, such as taking people to the airport. I have taken a number of people to the airport, and unless you have someone to take back, it's not as profitable as you would think.

The other day, I took a rider to the airport. The airport was twenty-six miles away. We were in city traffic, and the ride took almost an hour. The total charge was $29.80. Sounds great on the surface. Looks like I made $30 for that hour.

Let's break it down to reality. From the approximately $30, Uber always gets the first $1 per ride, which leaves $29. Uber then takes 20 percent of the $29, which equals $5.60.

$29 – $5.60 = $23.40 for the driver, minus any expenses. The total distance was fifty-two miles. It took almost an hour to get back, so two hours total were spent. $23.40 – $6 for gas = $17.40 for the driver for two hours of his or her time.

Like I said before, if you're lucky to be involved in a lot of surges, these numbers change, but the reality for most drivers is as shown. Making matters even worse for the drivers, Uber now has an app that tells the riders when the surge is over so they can call for a ride.

One last thing on the drivers' compensation: I drive about 200 to 250 miles per day for Uber, most of it in city traffic. That's over 50,000 miles per year. I can't even imagine the depreciation that vehicle is taking. It would be in the thousands per year—never mind the monthly servicing, new tires at least every year, brakes, and so forth. My conservative estimate of this cost would be about $1.25 per hour of driving.

If you're going to drive for a ride-share program, Lyft may be your better option. I also went through the Lyft application process. Lyft actually sends someone out to inspect your car. The inspector checked everything from tires and lights to signals. The inspector had me go on a ride to see what type of driver I was and discussed ways to help me in the drive-share business. Lyft also pays about 25 percent more than Uber, making it much more desirable for drivers.

I am a free-enterprise type of guy. But drivers have to get together somehow and force Uber to increase their compensation. Uber will just keep on bringing new drivers on board until the new drivers realize the true cost, making most likely less than minimum wage. As drivers leave, a new set of drivers comes on board, and the cycle continues.

I have picked up numerous former drivers who share the same understanding of the compensation package as I do.

The following are some of my actual compensation records.

This week, I spent 46.1 hours online with Uber. I made sixty-eight trips, and pay was $497.10. From this pay I have to subtract $3 per hour for gas. I am not even going to deduct $1.25 per hour for servicing and depreciation.

46.1 hours worked x $3 costs = $138.30 in fuel.

Subtract my costs of $138.30 from my $497.10 pay, and $358.80 was my real net profit.

To find my hourly rate, I divided $358.80 by the number of hours online, which was 46.1. This comes to $7.78 per hour.

Now I am going to show you my busiest week since I started driving for Uber. This week included $84 in surge pay.

I was 43.4 hours online. I made sixty-five trips and earned $549.40 in compensation.

My costs for gas were $3 per hour x 43.4 hours = $130.30.

$549.40 gross pay – $130.20 in costs = $414.20 net pay.

For my hourly rate, $414.20 divided by 43.3 hours online = $9.56 per hour.

If it wasn't for the surge pricing of $84, I would have made almost $2 less per hour, bringing my hourly rate to $7.56.

To sum it all up, the average driver will net, after costs, maybe $8 per hour. Remember, I haven't even taken off the costs of servicing or depreciation. If those calculations were taken into account, the true hourly rate would be even less.

The only reason I can think of why Uber reduced the drivers' compensation is that Uber wants to eliminate any competition, therefore increasing market share. This will enable Uber to take the company public, making it more profitable and appealing to investors.

As I have said earlier, these are my results. They may not reflect the results of other drivers. If you do plan on becoming a driver, keep track of your total costs—gas, wear and tear (deprecation), maintenance, oil, filter, tires, brakes, and so forth.

DRIVER SAFETY

Even though being an Uber driver is relatively safe, there are a lot of situations that arise that may be shocking to the public. The fact that Uber announced that Uber drivers are not allowed to carry protection just opened the door for those who wish to do harm.

The following are some stories I have received from Uber drivers, and they are mixed in with my own situations that I have come up against. Each story is a standalone, so you can open to any page in the book and find something interesting to read.

UBER STORIES

KIDNAPPED

A group called for an Uber for one of their friends who'd had way too much to drink. As a matter of fact, when she was placed in the car, the woman was already passed out.

As the Uber driver started to drive this passenger home, the woman came to and started to scream uncontrollably at the driver. "Who are you? Where you taking me?" The driver tried to explain to the woman that her friends had called for an Uber and placed her in the car to go home. Well, the woman wasn't having that for an answer. The passenger grabbed the driver by the hair, snapped his head back, and attempted to scratch his face, driving her fingers into his eyes, screaming at him, "You're not going to kill and rape me. I am going to kill you."

The driver managed to pull the car over and jumped out of the car. From the outside of the car, the driver told the woman to call her friends to verify the information. The woman called her friends and found out the driver was telling the truth. The woman was so upset with herself for acting like a crazy person. The driver told her it was okay and that he understood how it must have looked when she woke up.

The driver finished driving the woman home. As she climbed out of the car, she turned to the driver, apologized again for her behavior, and then gave him a twenty-dollar tip for his trouble.

CHANGE OF CLOTHES

A driver picked up a couple. The couple was very well dressed. The driver asked if they were going somewhere special. "Yes, we are going to a friend's wedding." As the driver was driving them to their destination, a strong, vile odor came up from the back seat. The smell was so bad the driver had to roll down his window. The smell penetrating every inch of the car. The smell was getting worse by the minute; the driver felt like throwing up. Then the woman asked the driver to drive her back to her house. The driver drove her home. As she was climbing out of the car, the driver noticed a large brown spot on the butt area of her white dress. It was obvious the woman had crapped in her pants. The woman returned about fifteen minutes later, and the driver continued to their destination. During that trip, not one word was said about the smell in the car.

MALL SHOPPING

A driver picked up a woman who wanted to go shopping at the mall. On the way, they struck up a friendly conversation about the insanity of life and how we all run around like a bunch of ants, never having time for anyone or anything, always too busy.

They arrived at the mall, and the woman asked the driver if he had time to walk around the mall with her for company. The driver thought about the conversation they had just had—how no one had any time for people anymore—and so he decided to go with the woman into the mall.

As they were walking around the mall, the woman walked into a men's clothing store. She turned to the driver and asked him if he would try some clothes on for her. She told him she had to buy a gift for someone who was his size and wanted to see how the clothes would look on.

The driver said, "Sure, why not?" There the driver was, trying on all these clothes for the woman. He was feeling a little bit stupid and embarrassed over the whole situation. The woman bought a pair of pants and a shirt, and they left the store.

The woman went into a nail salon and asked the driver if he ever had his nails professionally done. The driver said no. "Well, you don't know what you're missing. Sit down; you're having them done." Now the driver was sitting in a nail salon, having his nails done. He thought, "If only my friends could see me now."

After they had their nails done, the woman asked the driver to join her for a drink and appetizers. The driver again went along with the woman to the restaurant, where she ordered the food and drinks for both of them. The whole time the woman would not let the driver pay for anything.

Then the woman looked down at her watch and told the driver she had to go and meet a friend in the mall. She thanked him for his company and left him sitting there in the restaurant. The driver felt absolutely foolish over the whole ordeal. As he was leaving the mall, he looked around to make sure he didn't see that woman again. I said to the driver, "Look at it this way—you walked around the mall with this attractive woman, had your nails done, and had drinks and appetizers, all paid for by a woman. Most guys would think you are one lucky guy."

GAY PARTY INVITATION

A driver picked up two gay guys. They were on their way to a big gay party, celebrating the Supreme Court's decision to allow gay marriage.

The driver thought they must have just met because they were all over each other, french kissing and rubbing each other everywhere. The driver dared not look into his rearview mirror for fear they may have thought he was watching them as they made out like teenagers.

When the two finally came up for air, they started to tell the driver where they had first met and how in love they were with each other. They described how great the sex was between them.

The couple asked the driver if he had ever been with a man. The driver said no. "Well, you don't know what you're missing. Until you have another man give you oral sex, you will never know how great it can be."

The driver thought, "Why me?" The couple went on to describe anal sex and how it gave you the greatest orgasm. Now the driver couldn't believe the discussion he found himself involved in. "Why don't you come to the party tonight?" the couple asked. "We guarantee you will have a great time, but you must be open to all possibilities."

The driver told them he had to work but thanked them for the invitation. He dropped them off and said to himself, Well, that's another first, a personal invitation to a gay party. The driver told me he would have loved to have been a fly on the wall at that event.

PASSED OUT

A driver picked up a woman who was obviously intoxicated. As the driver turned to ask where she would like to go, he found her passed out in the back seat of the car. The driver asked her again and again where she wanted to go, but she wouldn't wake up. The driver told me he didn't know what to do. So he opened the door to the back seat and tried to shake the woman, but still she wouldn't wake up. The driver sat there for about an hour, hoping she would sleep some of it off enough to get an address. Finally he managed to get a response from her. She said to him, "Thank you for the ride," and tried to get out of the car. The driver said to her, "We haven't gone anywhere. You have been passed out for over an hour, and you failed to give me an address where you wanted to go." The woman gave the driver the address, and when they arrived at her house, the woman turned around and gave him a twenty-dollar tip for waiting. The driver was thankful for that tip because Uber really doesn't pay much of anything for waiting time.

THROW-UP TAG TEAM

A driver picked up a couple who were totally drunk. As the driver started to drive them to their destination, the woman said, "Stop the car. I am going to be sick." He stopped the car, and she got out and started to throw up. The woman then got back into the car. A quarter mile later, the man said, "Stop the car. I am going to be sick." The driver stopped the car, and the man got out and started to throw up. The man then got back in the car. The driver drove another quarter mile, and the woman yelled, "Stop the car. I am going to be sick." The driver stopped the car, and the woman got out and started to throw up again. The woman then got back in the car. The driver went about a mile, and the couple yelled, "Stop the car." The driver stopped the car, and they both got out, and both of them were now throwing up.

The driver thought, "There can't be anything left to throw up." Finally they both got back in the car, and the driver managed to arrive at their destination without any more episodes. The driver remarked to me how funny it was watching them trying to walk up their driveway to the house, bouncing off each other all the way.

GREY GOOSE FUN

A driver picked up a woman. They started making small talk. The discussion moved on to the subject of their favorite vodka. The woman said her favorite vodka was Grey Goose, but it was so expensive she hadn't been able to buy it. She stated she would do anything for a bottle of Grey Goose.

The woman then turned to the driver and said, "How would you like the best oral sex of your life?" The driver later told me he was shocked and really didn't know what to say.

Then she turned to the driver. "You buy me a bottle of Grey Goose, and I will make your day. It will be a day you will never forget." The driver sat there for a while and said to himself, Why not?

The driver told me he was nervous as hell. He pulled the car over to a deserted place. They both got into the back seat. She unzipped his pants and slowly pulled them down and took them off. He thought, "What if someone comes around while I have no pants on?" But that thought quickly disappeared when she took hold of his penis. The driver said to me she was definitely telling the truth when she said, "It will be the best oral sex you will ever have." The woman took her time. She licked the inside of his thighs, kissed his penis, and rode her tongue up and down the shaft. She acted like they were in a hotel somewhere, not caring that it was daylight and anyone could walk by. The driver said he was a nervous wreck through the whole thing. But the one thing he said to me was, "She never missed a drop."

Afterward the driver drove her to the liquor store and told her she could have whatever she wanted. She chose a 1.5-liter bottle of Grey Goose. The woman thanked the driver and walked away.

PRIVATE SCREENING

A driver went to a hotel and picked up three riders. The driver noticed one of the riders was a famous actor. The driver couldn't believe this actor was actually sitting in his car. The driver didn't acknowledge the actor out of respect for his privacy. The riders got in the vehicle and asked the driver to take them to the theater. On the way to the theater, the group pulled out scripts and started practicing their parts in a play. The driver asked, "What is the name of the play?" The group told the driver the name of the play. The play was well known, and the group told the driver how they traveled around the country performing the play in different cities.

The driver was overwhelmed with excitement. Here were three actors, one of them famous, practicing their parts on the way to the theater in his car. The driver thought, "Nobody is going to believe this one." So as he pulled up to the theater, the driver broke down and asked the actor for his autograph. The actor complied and gave his autograph to the driver.

BAD PART OF TOWN

A driver received a call from a rider. The call took him into a bad part of town. When the driver arrived, he called the rider to let him know that he was there. The rider didn't answer. The driver called again, leaving another message. The driver waited another ten minutes and then finally left because of a passenger no-show.

As the driver was driving out of the development, a guy waved him down. The driver assumed this was his rider. The driver asked the guy, "Did you call for an Uber?" The rider said yes. The rider, instead of getting into the car on the passenger side, either front or back seat, walked around the car, got in the car, and sat right behind the driver.

The driver said at that moment, a chill came over his body. The driver asked, "Where do you want to go?" The rider started to give him directions. It wasn't an address but street-by-street directions.

The driver said he felt the rider was trying to take him to a place where he would not be returning. Finally, the driver pulled over and said to the rider, "Either give me an address to where you want to go, or please leave my car."

At that moment, the rider moved forward and put his arm around the driver's neck, attempting a choke hold. The driver said he had his seat belt on and couldn't move. But he managed to slide his left hand between the rider's arm and his neck. It was enough to relieve a little of the pressure on his neck. The rider was squeezing with tremendous pressure on the driver's neck, screaming racial slurs at him: "Honkey; stupid cracker; now you're going to die." The driver could only pant for air because of the choke hold the rider had on him. He felt himself losing consciousness.

The driver told me all of a sudden, he said to himself, Do something. That was when he started punching behind him. As the rider tried to duck, the driver caught him with a number of punches to the face and the nose. The rider's nose started to bleed. The driver managed to grasp the rider by the hair. With his thumb, he found the rider's eye and drove his thumb deep into the rider's eye socket. Now, the driver started to yell back. The driver remembered yelling, "I am going to drive my thumb into your eye and rip your eye out." The driver kept yelling, "Now it's your turn to die. Now it's your turn to die. I feel your eyeball. It's almost out."

The driver felt the attacker's arm around his neck start to shake. Finally the rider let go and opened the door and ran.

The driver's neck was bruised, and he could barely talk. For the next few weeks, he had a very stiff neck. "The struggle for life and death that took place in my car never leaves me. I came so close to dying. Sometimes I just break down when the thoughts of that night flow into my mind."

I asked the driver why he didn't report it to the police. He said to me, "Are you kidding? First of all, they would never find him. If they did find him, somehow it would end up being my fault. If his eye was damaged in any way, then I would be sued. Haven't you been aware what's going on around the country?"

TILL DEATH DO US PART

The driver picked up an older couple. The couple was celebrating their fifty-fourth wedding anniversary. They told the driver to take them to the park where they used to go when they were dating. The driver drove them to the park. The couple asked the driver to wait.

The couple took out a blanket, walked down to the water's edge, laid the blanket down, and sat on the blanket. The driver watched the couple just gazing out over the water. The couple then started to embrace each other. The driver stated that the couple began to kiss and make out like teenagers. The driver watched as they massaged each other's bodies, stopping at all the right places. The couple then covered themselves with the blanket. The driver swore they were being intimate.

Finally they returned to the car, got in the back seat, and sat there like nothing had happened.

The driver said he couldn't help himself asking the question, "How do you still manage to have all this love and passion after all these years?"

The drive said to me, "They told me it hadn't always been like this. They had gone through some terrible times where they both felt they didn't love each other anymore and actually contemplated divorce. But as they looked around at people they knew getting divorces, they saw the destruction of families, finances, and children.

"Then, when their friends remarried, in most cases it ended up worse off than their first marriages, with multiple parents and four sets of grandparents, and the reality was the new spouses would truly never accept our children, our flesh and blood, as their own. Then the couple thought, 'What's going to happen with future grandchildren? This divorce will cause havoc for generations to come, with children not feeling connected to any family. Just look around now. That's why we have such social chaos. The breakdown of the family has been shown to be the root cause.'

"The couple explained, 'We decided that if we were going to stay true to our oath, which we swore to each other, God, and all the witnesses at our wedding, we had to come up with some agreed-upon guidelines for us to commit to and follow.

1) We both must agree upon any issue before action can be taken.
2) If we can't mutually agree, we agree to disagree without malice.
3) We are not allowed to criticize or judge each other.
4) We allow each other to do what he or she loves without feeling left out.
5) We allow each other privacy, such as changing, showering, and other personal functions. This keeps the passion alive.
6) We must always show respect for each other and never indulge in any name calling.

"'I know this sounds like a legal contract, but if any situation is going to survive, there have to be rules to follow. Once we made these commitments to each other, everything changed. Knowing divorce wasn't an option, we started to see the person we married again. Our love grew stronger than ever. That's why God is against divorce. God, with great wisdom, knew couples would eventually find what they thought they lost in each other.'"

The driver then reflected back to his own personal situation with his ex-wife. He thought maybe if there had been rules such as those followed by this older couple, he might have never been divorced. But then again, both parties would have had to agree to follow them.

HOT-HEADED LATINO

I picked up a couple who went on to tell me about this Uber driver who threatened and intimated them to the point where they called the Uber head office and filed a complaint.

The driver picked them up, and the couple entered their destination in the app. When they arrived at their destination, the couple asked the driver if they could be driven somewhere else. The driver responded, "No problem." He told them to just tell him where to go and not to bother entering the destination into the app. So the couple started to give him the directions. The driver got confused, and the couple thought he really didn't understand English. They almost crashed into other vehicles on more than one occasion. Then the driver turned around and started to yell at the couple, calling them fucking assholes, saying, "Why didn't you enter the directions?" The driver blamed them for almost getting into numerous vehicular accidents. The driver started to drive erratically. The couple feared for their safety.

The couple yelled, "Stop the car! Stop the car! Let us out." The driver by now was screaming at them, using every swear word known in the English and Spanish languages. The couple by now knew for sure he didn't understand English and was totally out of control.

Finally, the driver stopped the car. The couple got out of the car and slammed the door shut. The driver jumped out of the car and started to chase them down the street, telling the guy he was going to fuck him up the ass, calling him a gay faggot. The couple ran to a crowd of people and put their hands up in the air, asking for help. The couple said everyone started to see the driver's crazed behavior. The driver then turned around and left.

The couple told me the car itself didn't seem to meet the standards they'd had seen with other drivers' vehicles. The car had pins holding up the interior roof. There was an odor in the car. The car looked like it hadn't been washed in months. The car definitely did not meet Uber standards.

DRIVER FROM INDIA

I picked up a woman, and as we were driving to her destination, she started telling me about another Uber driver. Now, this woman was attractive—she had long blond hair, she was in great shape, and she was about thirty-five years old.

The woman went on to tell me that her Uber driver told her he was from India. The driver started by commenting on how beautiful she was. He started to ask very personal questions, such as "Are you married? Are you happily married? Do you have any children? What does your husband do?" The questions just went on and on. She was feeling very uncomfortable.

Then the driver said, "You're so beautiful. You really got me excited." The driver asked her to look up front and see what he was doing. The driver said he couldn't help himself. She told me, "I think he was masturbating and wanted me to watch." This fear came over her—what should she do? Jump out of a moving car? Call 911 on her phone? But then she thought, "If I call 911, what might the driver do to me?"

Finally she arrived at home and got out of the car. She then went on the Uber app and gave the driver a five-star rating. I said, "Why would you do that?" She told me she did it out of fear; he knew where she lived, and he might return. I told her the driver could not see the rating you gave him. I suggested she call or e-mail Uber and file a complaint to have this driver removed from driving with Uber. But she would have no part of that out of fear.

I told the woman Uber should not be hiring drivers where you couldn't get a full detailed criminal background check. That was the problem with taking a cab in a major city. Most of the drivers were from countries where you could not do a full background check. All the information you would receive on a background check was what they had done since moving to the U.S.A. That was just not good enough.

GAY DRIVER

I picked up this young guy who was maybe twenty years old. This was his first Uber ride. He went on to tell me that his friends used it all the time, but he had been a little nervous to use Uber. I asked why. He said it was because of what had happened to a friend of his.

"What happened to your friend?" I asked. He went on to tell me that his friend had had too much to drink and called for an Uber to pick him up. The Uber arrived, and he got in the car. The driver, he could tell, looked gay, but that didn't bother him. The driver started to ask him a lot of questions, such as "Do you have a girlfriend?" and "Have you ever been with a girl?"

The young man said, "My friend really didn't think much of the questions. He thought the driver was just being friendly. My friend had a lot to drink, and fell asleep or passed out in the back seat of the car. When he awoke, the driver had the young man's pants down and was attempting to perform oral sex on him. At the same time, the driver had his own pants down and was masturbating while attempting to perform oral sex on the passenger. My friend said, 'What the fuck are you doing?' The driver said, 'You were so cute. I just couldn't resist.'"

I asked the young man, "What did your friend do?"
"He just jumped out of the car and ran."
"Did he report it to Uber?"
"No, it was too embarrassing of a situation to talk about."

UNFRIENDLY DRIVER

I picked up a couple. They came walking out from their home and looked in the window. They then proceeded to get in the car. I said, "How are you guys today?"

"Better now."

I said, "What do you mean?" They went on to tell me how they had had the Uber driver from hell a week ago and were debating whether to ever use Uber rides again.

I said, "What happened?"

"Well, when we got into the driver's car, the driver said, 'It must be nice to live in a house like that.' We said, 'Thank you. We really enjoy living there.' Then he said where he came from, nobody lived like that. Then I said, 'Oh, where are you from?' He said, 'Somalia.'"

The driver had then started to question them: "What do you do for a living to make that kind of money to live there?"

The couple had said, "It's none of your business."

It was obvious to the couple that the driver had been extremely angry. "He was mumbling under his breath all kinds of words in a language we couldn't understand. Needless to say, the rest of the trip was a frightening ride from hell. His driving was totally erratic—he was going around corners too fast. I felt like the car was going to flip over. He was not stopping at stop signs, speeding through traffic, and changing lanes without even looking. When we finally arrived at our destination, he slammed the brakes on, throwing us forward in the seats, and screamed at us to get out of his car. We opened the door and jumped out of the car, ran, and found a place to hide. We were now afraid he might try to run us over."

The driver continued, "I told them the same thing I told the other people—you have to file a complaint with Uber. Uber doesn't know about these crazy drivers unless you tell them. I got the same response: 'He knows where we live.'"

I know I keep repeating myself, but you tell me how Uber can do a background check on this driver and review a DOT driving record. I am sure one doesn't exist where he came from in Somalia.

REPTILIAN DRIVER

I picked up a young guy who was about eighteen years old. I was driving him to his part-time job at the movie theater. On the way, he started to tell me how this was his second Uber ride ever. But after the first ride, he thought he would never take another one. I asked him why. He went on to tell me how the other driver had started telling him about the Reptilians and how they controlled the world.

The driver had gone on about how every historical document had references to the Reptilians. The recorded history of these Reptilians went back over thirty-five hundred years. The Sumerian clay tablets found in the middle of Iraq in the middle of the nineteenth century told the same story.

The driver told the guy that these ancient tablets talked about a race of gods from another world who had brought advanced knowledge to the planet and interbred with humans to create hybrid bloodlines. By this time, the guy told me, he had been freaking out and didn't know what to do.

The driver had gone on to tell him how George Bush was mentioned more than anyone else in the tablets and had been seen shape-shifting (this is how they went back and forth between Reptilian and human), that all the people at the top were related in some way and controlled politics, banking, military, media, and so on.

The rider by now had been convinced he was riding with a major nut job and might not make it out of this vehicle in one piece. Finally the driver had reached his destination and let him out. The rider had felt such relief being out of that car.

For your interest, I researched the topic of Reptilians on earth and was shocked by the millions of people that believe in them. In addition, there is ancient historical documentation you might find interesting or disturbing. You be the judge.

TRANSVESTITE DRIVER

I picked up a couple who told me about their first Uber experience. They had called for an Uber, and while they were waiting for the car, they had followed the car on their phone. They had looked at the picture of their driver. It had been a woman with long blond hair. When the Uber had arrived, they had noticed the woman had long red hair. So the couple had said to the woman, "You changed your hair color."

The woman had responded with the deepest male voice, "Yes, I thought I would go red. I have been blond long enough—needed a change." The couple had been totally shocked by this deep male voice and realized it wasn't a woman but a man dressed up as a woman. The couple told me they had felt a little uneasy with the whole thing and didn't know whether to get in the car or not. They had finally decided to take the ride anyway. On the way to their destination, the driver had tried to make small talk with the couple. The couple said it had been difficult listening to this woman talking with the deep voice of a man. But the driver had been pleasant enough—it was just the initial shock factor that they had to adjust to. After that, everything had been fine.

TATTOO GIRL

A driver picked up a girl with tattoos all over her body. The woman was beautiful, with long black hair and large dark-brown eyes, and it was obvious she kept herself in great shape. She was wearing a skintight, short-cut black dress. As the driver was driving her to her location, the girl started telling the driver how she'd just moved there from out of state a couple of months ago. The girl went on to say that she'd met this woman bartender who'd taken her out the back of the bar, where they had smoked some pot.

Later, the bartender had invited her back to her house for a drink. "We got to her home, where we started drinking. The next thing I knew, she was trying to kiss me. I told her I had never been with a woman before. The bartender, who was a large woman, proceeded to force me to perform oral sex on her. I tried to push her back, but she was big and strong. She pulled my clothes off and hers. She held me down and pushed her pussy into my face and said, 'Lick it.' I finally did and found out it turned me on—I liked it. What is really crazy is I ended up moving in with her and her two gay male roommates."

The driver said, "The girl told me when the two gay guys were having sex, they made so much noise that on a number of occasions, she would walk in their room and tell them to shut up. The girl said when she and her girlfriend had sex, it was nice and quiet. They didn't yell and scream."

The driver couldn't believe the conversation he was having with this woman. As the driver was pulling up to her destination, the passenger turned around and said, "You know, I really don't mind who I have sex with, as long as he or she is a nice person." Then she turned around and said to the driver, "I think you're a nice person," and put her hand on his thigh. The driver looked her in the eyes, and then she grabbed his crotch and proceeded to unzip his pants. The driver didn't know what to do, so he just let her do whatever she wanted. She slipped her hand in his pants, took out his penis, and performed oral sex on him in the front seat of the car, on the street, as people were walking by. When she finished, she got out of the car like nothing had happened and thanked the driver for the ride.

TIRE CHANGE

A driver picked up two guys. They were going to the airport and were tight on time. So the driver loaded up their luggage, and off they went to the airport. The driver was speeding down the highway so the passengers wouldn't be late for their flight. All of a sudden, it felt like they'd hit something on the road. Then the car started shaking, and the driver knew he had blown a tire. As they pulled over to the side of the highway, the driver turned and said to the riders, "If we wait for AAA, you'll miss your flight. If we wait for another Uber, you will miss your flight. We only have one chance to get there on time. Let's all work together and change the tire ourselves."

So that's what they did. Everyone got out and did something. Within six or seven minutes, the tire was changed, and they got to the airport on time for their flights.

ANGRY HUSBAND

A driver picked up a woman and took her to the grocery store. When she finally came back to the car, it looked like she had brought enough groceries for a month. The driver helped her load everything into the car and then drove her home. When they arrived at her home, the driver began to help the woman carry her groceries into the house. As the driver was placing the groceries on the kitchen counter, a man walked in from another room and said to his wife, "So this is the guy you're fucking." The driver was shocked. He didn't know what to do, so he tried to explain that he was just a driver helping her bring her groceries in.

The man said, "You expect me to believe that bullshit? You're not the first one who has been fucking my wife. But I do know one thing—you will never be with her or any other woman again."

He opened the cupboard and pulled out a gun and then placed the barrel of the gun on the driver's forehead. The man said, "I hope that piece of ass was worth your life, because now you're going to die."

The driver was in full-blown panic mode, trying to tell her husband, "You have the wrong guy. Look, I am an Uber driver. Look at my phone. It's my job."

At that moment, the wife stepped in and tried to defuse the situation. The wife told the husband, "Look at this driver. He is a loser, driving people around for a living. You know me; I could never let some loser like that ever touch me. That driver would be the last person I would ever consider being with."

The driver said that while the wife was trying to calm down her husband, she waved for him to go. He slipped out the door, ran to his car, and sped out of there. The driver told me that you don't know what fear is until something like that happens to you. "My heart was pounding so hard that I thought I was going to die right there. I hate to admit it, but I wet myself during the ordeal. I learned a valuable lesson that day. Never go into someone's home. You just don't know what to expect."

WRONG PEOPLE

A driver received a call to pick someone up at the airport. The driver called the rider back, confirmed her name, and told her what kind of car he was driving and that he would have his lights on. The driver drove to the pickup area, and a woman flagged him down. The driver stopped and opened the trunk of the car to help a couple put their luggage away.

The driver told me, "I thought to myself, this must one of their first vacations, because they had so much luggage." Finally they got everything in the car, and the driver started to drive them to their destination. There was no destination input into Uber, so the driver asked, "Where you are going?" The driver was told to drive to a well-known resort. The driver started talking to the couple. The couple told them they were from Tennessee, and this was their first trip away without the children.

While everyone was talking, the driver received a phone call. It was from a rider who asked the driver, "Where in the hell are you going? You left the airport without me, you dumb ass."

Then the driver turned around and asked the riders, "Did you call for an Uber?" They said no; the resort had sent a car to pick them up.

The driver continued telling his story. "I said, 'What kind of car?'" Well, it turned out the car was the same model and color as the driver's. To make matters even more unbelievable, both women had the same name. What were the odds? The driver had picked up the wrong people. When the driver told the riders about what happened, everyone just started to laugh.

"I told the rider on the phone I would be right back to get her. Then the rider said, 'You all think it's funny, you fuckin' loser.' The yelling and swearing by that woman were insane."

You would think the driver had killed her dog or something. It was so loud that the passengers in the back seat of the car overheard the whole situation. Well, no one could believe the language this woman was using. "Obviously she didn't want me to come back and get her." The driver returned to the airport and let the wrong riders out. As they were leaving, they gave the driver a twenty-dollar tip and wished him luck.

POSSIBLE TERRORIST

A driver picked up a rider who was carrying all kinds of boxes and bags. The stuff filled the trunk and the back seat of the car. The driver said to him, "It looks like you're moving."

The drive continued, "The rider said he had just arrived from Pakistan and had me drive him to a room he rented. So I asked him if he had a job waiting for him when he arrived. He said, 'No, I will have to find one.'" The driver asked him what he did. The rider said he was in banking and was working in the Middle East.

The driver said it must be very dangerous to work over there. The rider said, "We all have to die sometime, and I am not afraid of death. Quite the contrary—I am looking forward to it."

"We continued talking about the Middle East. The rider said the United States should not be there. 'They are an intruder. Let the countries work out their own problems.'"

The driver said the rider had a bad odor coming from him. Maybe he hadn't showered in days, but it was a terrible smell. The driver was doing his best not to gag during the ride to the room the rider had rented.

The driver changed the subject to banking. He asked the rider, "And what do you think about the Greek banking situation?"

The rider said, "What situation is that?"

"Well," the driver told the rider, "Greece has closed their banks for ten days, and people can't access their money." The rider said that he hadn't been following the news and wasn't aware of the situation. The driver continued to talk about loans and other financial matters and soon realized this guy knew nothing about banking. He thought, "He is not here for a job at a bank."

Finally they arrived at the destination. After the rider had left, it took a whole can of Febreze to get the smell out of the car.

APARTMENT GIRL

This driver would pick this girl up about three times a week and take her to work. He said they became quite friendly. She was twenty-six years old, and he was in his fifties, but they had a connection. One day she asked him if he would like to come to her apartment sometime for a drink. The driver said that would be nice. So they set a time on Sunday where he would go up and hang out with this girl for a while.

The driver told me he didn't really know what to expect, but on the chosen Sunday, he went up to see her. When he walked into the apartment, there was very little furniture in the place—just a couch and chair but no tables of any kind and nowhere to sit in order to eat.

She made him a cup of coffee. Out of the blue, she told him how much she hated men. The driver asked why.

"Every man has let me down, especially my father, who was never around when I was growing up. Oh, he would come around once in a while, just to try to have sex with me. Any boyfriend I ever had ended up cheating on me. I have not gone out with a man in four years. I hate to be touched by anybody."

The driver asked, "Why did you invite me up here if you hate men?"

She told the driver it was because he seemed really nice and that she felt comfortable with him.

The driver thanked her for that comment and told her he had to go. Before he left, she gave him sixty dollars. The driver didn't want to take it, but she insisted. She knew the driver had lost that amount of money the two hours he was off the Uber app. The driver left and just couldn't believe what had just happened. The driver thought, "Crazy parents don't realize the long-term effects their behavior has on their children. Here's a young girl ruined for life."

LOST BRA

This is a story told to an Uber driver by a woman rider he picked up. The woman got into his car and started to tell the Uber driver about the last Uber ride she had taken. The woman said she had been drunk when the driver had picked her up. When they had arrived at her house, the driver had gotten out and opened the door for the woman. Being drunk, she had tripped as she got out of the car. The driver had caught her. Their eyes had met, and they had started kissing. Then she had taken off her shirt and bra, and they had had sex on the hood of his car.

    The woman had taken the driver upstairs to her apartment and continued with the sexual encounter. Afterward, the woman had asked the driver to go home because she didn't like anyone sleeping over. The driver had left. The next day, the woman had called the driver because he still had her bra. The driver had come back to her house to return the bra, where they again had sex in her bed. But this time she had told the driver not to call her or come back around because he was useless in bed. Of course, the Uber driver hearing this story was shocked by the direct honesty in the way she spoke.

THREE BROKEN PHONES

A driver picked someone at a phone sales store. The rider said he had had to replace his phone. Three days later, the driver picked up the same guy at the same phone store, and the rider said he had had to replace his phone. A few days later, the driver went back to the same phone store, where he picked up the same guy, who said he had had to replace his phone.

The Uber driver remarked, "Wow, that's three phone replacements in just over a week. Are they all defective?" The rider said no, the first phone his dog had destroyed; the second phone he had dropped in the toilet; and the third phone his girlfriend had thrown at him because she had caught him with another woman, and it had smashed.

The rider said, "It's not going to break anymore because I purchased this ninety-dollar case for it that's indestructible."

The driver said, "Well, it's too bad you never thought of that with the first phone."

LUNCH, ANYONE?

An Uber driver received a call for pickup. The driver went to the location and called the rider, letting her know he was out front waiting. The rider said, "I will be right out." Ten minutes later, she still hadn't come out, so the driver called her again. Again the woman apologized and said she would be right out. The driver waited another ten minutes and still no rider. He called again, and again she said, "I will be right out." The driver waited another few minutes and called again—this time, no answer. He called another couple of times—no answer. As the driver was getting ready to leave, the woman came out of the house. She got in the car and acted like nothing had happened and asked the driver to take her to a bakery. The woman went into the bakery came back a minute later with the biggest apple fritter you could image. She gave the apple fritter to the driver and said, "This is for you. I will be right back." Then she went back into the bakery.

The driver said he felt like a little child who had been given a reward for being patient. The driver sat there eating his apple fritter and realized the woman still hadn't come out. He called her again, and she came out and asked the driver to drive her home. The driver said, "You were in there a long time."

The woman turned and said to him, "I am a slow eater, but my lunch was delicious." The driver dropped her off and couldn't believe what had just happened. He had ended up waiting for her while she had lunch, and Uber paid almost nothing for wait time.

TRANSGENDER

A driver received a call to pick a rider up at a coffee shop. When the driver arrived, he called the woman to let her know he was out front. The woman came out and sat right beside him in the passenger seat. The driver was initially shocked. It wasn't a woman or a man. The person had makeup on, long hair, and breast implants and was wearing high heels with a full beard.

The driver had never seen anything like it before. The rider went on to say that he/she couldn't wait to get back to San Francisco. The driver asked why. The rider said it was because there everyone stared at him/her, and in San Francisco, he/she was not even noticed. He/she just fit in with the crowd.

Another transgender person that this driver had picked up was similar to the first one, only this one had half his body as a man and half as a woman. This person had long blond hair on half of his head, with full makeup on half of his face. The other half of his head had short hair and no makeup, with half of a beard. The person would switch between a male voice and a female voice. All in all, the transgender people were very nice, polite, and respectful.

POSSIBLE DRUG RUN

A driver picked up a rider. The rider had him drive to a check-cashing store and told the driver to wait. The rider came out of the check-cashing store, jumped in the car, and said, "Hurry—go to McDonald's. I have to meet someone there." They arrived at McDonald's. The rider told the driver to wait. The driver saw the rider talking to what looked like shady characters. The rider came back and said, "Go to the supermarket." They arrived at the supermarket, and the rider told the driver to wait. The rider came out with what looked like a money order in his hand. The rider then asked the driver take him to a variety store in a bad part of town. The rider asked the driver to wait. The rider came out and said, "Drive back to McDonald's," where he met the same people. The rider then told the driver to take him back to where he had been picked up.

URINE IN CAR

A driver picked up a woman. She stumbled getting into the back seat of the car. The driver realized she was very drunk. On the way to her destination, the driver noticed she was pulling down her shorts and underwear. Before the driver could say anything, she started to urinate in the back seat of the car. The driver yelled, "Excuse me, what are you doing?"

The rider yelled back, "What are you doing in the women's washroom?"

The driver was furious with the whole event but could do very little at the time.

Because she was so drunk, he dared not go near her in any way. Who knew what she might say, considering she thought she was in the washroom? The driver just continued to the destination and dropped her off. The driver said he had to call it a night and went home to attempt to remove the urine and smell from his car.

WINE OPENER

A driver picked up a woman and took her shopping at the supermarket. When they arrived back at her home, he helped carry in the groceries and then left. About five minutes later, he received a phone call. It was the same woman he had just taken shopping. She told him she forgot to get a wine opener and asked if he could please go pick one up for her and bring it back.

The driver agreed, picked up the wine opener, and took it back to her home. When he arrived, the door was open. He knocked, and she said, "Just leave the opener on the kitchen table." As he was about to leave, she asked him to have a drink with her. He said he couldn't; he was working. The woman wasn't giving up. The woman started to cry, telling the driver how she had just broken up with her boyfriend a few months ago and was having a difficult time with the breakup. The driver decided to stay and have a few drinks with her.

After a few drinks, the woman left the room and came back with a see-through outfit on. The driver didn't know what to think or do. She came up to him, placed her hand on his knee, and asked the driver if he found her attractive. The driver said, "Yes, you're beautiful." The woman then moved her hand to his crotch, unzipped his pants, took out his penis, and started performing oral sex on him. The driver couldn't believe what was happening. He thought to himself, "I thought this stuff just happens in movies or what you read in *Penthouse*."

The woman stopped and started taking all his clothes off. She took him by the hand into her bedroom, where she pushed him down on the bed. Without him really noticing, she managed to handcuff him to the bed. The driver now started to freak out in his head. "Was she going to kill him—was there a man in the next room?" All these crazy thoughts kept running through his mind. He was beating himself up for being so stupid as to stay.

Then she climbed on top of him and started to ride him like she was on a horse. Harder and harder, she drove herself on top of him. The woman seemed angry as she kept pounding him into the mattress. Finally she stopped, climbed off, uncuffed him, and said, "Please shut the door when you leave." Then she walked out of the bedroom. There he was in some strange woman's house, thinking of all the negative things that could happen—she could claim rape; her husband could find him; maybe she had some form of VD and wanted to spread it. What the hell had he been thinking?

SURROUNDED IN THE HOOD

A driver dropped off a rider in a bad part of town. After he dropped him off, the driver stopped to rate the rider. Within seconds, the car was surrounded by a number of people who started to use a lot of foul language. The driver said, "I am just an Uber driver—just dropping off a passenger." But it didn't help; they wanted him out of their neighborhood. The group started to rock the car. Then they all went to one side of the car, attempting to flip it over. The driver thought, "If I pull away, I might hurt someone; if I don't pull away, I am going to be hurt."

Just as they had the side of the car off the ground, the driver put the petal to the metal and just managed to get away before he went over. The driver told me that almost every time he went into that area, something seemed to happen. The driver decided he would not go back into that area again, period. I reminded the driver that if he refused to go into that neighborhood on an ongoing basis, Uber would cut him off. The driver came back and said, "My life is more important than being cut off by Uber."

MASS MURDERER

A driver picked up a rider in a run-down mobile-home community. The rider got into the car and sat in the front seat next to the driver. The rider's clothes were dirty. He had a bad odor radiating from him, and his hair was dirty, messy, and unkempt.

As the driver was driving the rider to his destination, they encountered heavy traffic. Then the rider said, "Every third person."

The driver said, "What do you mean, 'every third person'?"

"The earth is so overcrowded. We don't need all these people taking up space, destroying good farmland to build houses, and causing pollution—and for what? For people that come here from other countries, especially illegals." Then he started to recite all the crime statistics on illegals. "Fifty percent of all murders in Texas are caused by illegals, seventy percent of all arrest warrants in LA County are for illegals, and thirty-five percent of the prison population are illegals. Illegals cost us one hundred and fifty billion dollars a year."

He said if the government didn't act, the people should rise up and take care of this cancer on society. The driver didn't know what to say; this vagrant-looking guy seemed to know what he was talking about. Finally they arrived at the rider's destination. His destination was a psychological clinic—a treatment center for the mentally ill.

SAVED BY UBER DRIVER

A driver arrived at a downtown street location to pick up a rider. As the driver pulled up, he witnessed two guys harassing another man. You could tell the person being harassed was trying to get away from his attackers. The driver started to beep his horn, hoping to scare the attackers away. But that didn't work. Now the attackers were kicking the man while he was on the ground.

The driver jumped out of the car and ran toward the attackers, screaming, "The police are on the way." Meanwhile, the police hadn't even been called. The attackers stopped kicking the guy on the ground and turned their attention to the Uber driver.

The attackers said to him, "Think you're a tough guy?"

The driver knew he had to be forceful in his voice and show no fear. The driver said to the attackers, "Why don't you come over here and find out how tough I am?" The driver told me he was trying to call their bluff.

Well, they started to approach him. The driver said, "Come on—let's go. I need a workout." The attackers then started to use all kinds of foul language, but the driver wasn't backing down. The attackers turned around and started to laugh as they took off, calling the driver a pussy and saying they weren't going to waste their time on such a loser.

The driver went over to the rider and helped him up and asked if he was okay. The rider was okay, and the driver drove him home. On the way to his home, the driver told the guy he should call the police. The rider said, "No, thanks. I know who these guys are, and if I tell anybody, they will find me."

TWO GIRLS

It was New Year's Eve, one of the busiest days of the year. Everyone you picked up at the beginning of the night was simply beautiful—the women had their hair done and wore makeup and stunning dresses, and guys were in tuxes with combed hair and shiny shoes.

About 2:00 a.m., a driver picked up two girls who he thought couldn't be twenty-one years old. They climbed into the back seat of the car, hair messed up, makeup smeared all over their faces, drunk. As the driver started to drive them to their destination, one of the girls sitting directly behind him started to rub his shoulders and said, "You must be tired after driving all night." The driver said that was true and that he'd be heading home after he dropped them off. The girl then started to kiss his neck. Just as the driver turned to say something to the girls, the two girls started to kiss each other. They went from French kissing each other to lying down in the back seat. The driver glanced back, and one had her head under the dress of the other. There was a lot of screaming and moaning coming from the two of them. The driver could only imagine what was going on. Obviously they must have forgotten they were in the back seat of an Uber.

The driver announced loudly, "We're here. Time to go." The girls sat up, straightened their dresses, and fixed their hair. They thanked the driver for the ride and got out of the car.

PREGNANT WOMAN

This story is one we can all relate to. A driver went to pick a woman up. The woman climbed into his car and was obviously very pregnant. The driver asked where she wanted to go. She said, "To the hospital"; her water had just broken.

The driver freaked out quietly in his own mind; he thought he might have to deliver this baby in the car. The driver was racing to the hospital, praying he would get her there on time, running through stop signs and red lights if nobody was coming. The woman started to go into painful labor, screaming with the contractions. Fear had now taken over the driver's body. He thought, "Who in the hell would ever call an Uber to take you to the hospital after your water breaks?"

But he was there now, in this situation; he had to keep it together for the woman's sake and show no fear. He kept on trying to carry on a conversation between contractions. The contractions were coming faster now; he knew, after having three children, what that meant. A beautiful sight came into view—the hospital emergency entrance. The driver pulled in, ran into the emergency room, and called for help. The hospital staff came out and took the woman into the hospital. The driver said the feeling of relief was overwhelming, and it took him a couple of hours to calm down after that situation.

LOTTERY TICKET

A driver picked up a couple from out of town. You could tell the two had been drinking. As the driver was driving them to their destination, which was less than a mile away, the man asked the driver to stop at a convenience store. Before the man got out of the car to go into the store, the couple started to tell the driver about their relationship.

They were both married and had slipped away from their spouses for a night of fun and sex. They worked at the same small company, and if their relationship was found out, both of them would be fired. The couple went on to say how they sneaked around the office and had sex in various parts of the office. The most thrilling time was when they'd had sex on their boss's desk.

The couple started to laugh. The driver asked, "What are you laughing about?"

"Well, the woman said every time I go into his office, I remember the time we had sex on his desk. Now it's very hard for me to look at him, sitting behind it, being so serious when he talks to me."

"But there was one time that was the ultimate thrill—my boyfriend was working at his desk. I crawled under his desk and started to give him oral sex. Then the boss walked up and started to talk to him while I was giving him oral sex. You had to be there in the moment—talk about fear and excitement at the same time."

The driver said, "If it's okay for Bill Clinton and Monica, it should be okay for you."

At that moment, the man got out of the car and went into the store. He came out and gave the driver a lottery ticket. The driver said, "You didn't have to do that."

"Well," the man said, "you have been an incredible driver, listening to all our crazy stories without passing judgment on us."

As the driver went to drop them off, the girl turned around and gave the driver a twenty-dollar tip for a four-dollar ride and said, "Thanks again." The driver told me it was quite the one-mile ride that he would never forget.

NO RELIGION HERE

It was Sunday morning. A driver picked up his rider and casually said, "On your way to church?"

The rider went a little crazy. "What, religion! The biggest control of a mass population ever conceived. There is a big difference between religion and God."

The driver thought, "What have I gotten myself into?"

"Religion persuades people that they are insignificant and powerless, so they have to live their lives in accordance with the church doctrine. They don't have the ability to think for themselves or create and control their own lives.

"Religion has been one of the best tools for imparting fear into people of a judgmental God. Religion tells them, 'Believe in what I preach found in one book or belief system.' If not, they are going to hell.

"Different religions are great for dividing people and ruling through self-righteous, interreligious conflict. Do you really believe the nonsense they shove down your throat? All they're after is control.

"Think logically for a moment. Do you honestly believe this superbeing, whose energy flows through everything, would get upset with you if you didn't use a certain religion to contact him? Every religion says it is the only way to God. Religion was created by man for power, control, and money. It has caused more death on this planet than anything else."

The driver was so glad when he pulled up at the rider's destination and learned a valuable lesson in the process: never talk religion or politics again with anyone.

THREESOME, ANYONE?

A driver picked up a couple who had the driver take them to a number of sex-toy stores. When the driver pulled up to the second sex-toy store, the couple asked the driver to come in with them.

The driver went in and was amazed at the different toys people used. The driver had never been into one of these stores before. They left that store and went to another one. By this time it was about 6:00 p.m.

The couple asked the driver to drive them home. When they arrived at home, the couple asked the driver to come in for a drink. The driver thought, "Hell, why not?" The woman made him a vodka martini, and they sat around sharing their experiences in the sex-toy stores, talking about all the gadgets and what they were used for.

Just then, the woman got up and went into the other room. The driver never really thought anything about it. Then the man got up and went into the other room. There the driver was, sitting alone in their house, feeling very awkward. At that moment, the woman walked out of the other room totally naked. The driver told me she had the body of a supermodel, something you would only see in magazines.

The woman went behind the driver and started to rub his neck and then started to kiss it. She moved her hand slowly down his body, massaging his chest, down to his groin. The driver said that between the alcohol and this woman massaging him everywhere, you could imagine that he felt totally out of control. The woman then took all his clothes off.

Now both of them were totally nude. She took his hand and walked him into the other room. Here's where he got the shock of his life. The man was lying in the bed totally nude also. "Now what?" the driver thought. He had never been in this type of situation before. The woman had him lie down and started performing oral sex on him, while at the same time the man was having intercourse with her. The driver didn't really want to go into any more detail; he felt embarrassed and ashamed about the whole ordeal. The things he did in that room that night will stay in that room. But he did say it was something that would follow him for the rest of his life.

THE PREPPER

A driver picked up a rider and was taking him to the airport. The driver asked, "So where are you headed?"

The rider said, "To a prepper convention."

The driver said, "What is a prepper?"

The rider said, "It's about being ready for any calamity that may happen." The rider went on to say he couldn't understand families who refused to do anything about their personal well-being and safety.

"As a matter of fact, I think it's totally irresponsible to be completely unprepared to feed your children and provide them with water and shelter.

"We as preppers believe in personal responsibility and self-reliance. Do you honestly think the government is going to protect everyone if we are hit with some major crisis? Do you remember Hurricane Katrina? Have you been watching the news lately? We are headed for an economic meltdown. Look at Greece. They are attempting to place a bandage over a disaster. Chinese markets have dropped almost thirty percent, and the only reason they haven't dropped further is because China stopped all trading on its markets. Puerto Rico is bankrupt. Soon to follow are Russia, Italy, and Spain. Why do you think Russia is causing trouble in Europe? It's to take Russia's population's mind off the reality of their economy. Russia needs oil to be around a hundred dollars per barrel to keep their economy going."

The driver told me that this rider was one of the most knowledgeable people he had ever met.

The rider went on to say, "We have let in almost two million Muslims into this country over the last ten years alone for a total of eight million. They did a survey of American Muslims; eighty-two percent want sharia law, not US law, and forty percent of American Muslims believe violence against nonbelievers is okay. People must convert to Islam by any means necessary.

"How long do you think it's going to be before they start a war within our own country? The Muslims are waiting; they are moving into all parts of government and society. Remember Fort Hood?

"The United States is shortly going to be twenty trillion dollars in debt we can't tax our way out of. The American government is going to end up taking money from the population's bank accounts to help pay for the debt, as they did in some other countries.

"The next president, no matter who it is, will not be able to repair the damage caused by the Obama administration."

The driver went on to tell me that if I was smart, I should take all my money out of my 401(k) and any other savings accounts and only keep in the bank what I needed to pay my monthly bills. The US government had already come out telling the population they did not own their bank accounts.

Finally, they got to the airport. The driver thanked the rider for the information and wished him luck. The driver told me that he had looked up online a lot of the things the rider was telling him.

It seemed most of what he was saying was true. The driver said, "I am left now with a very nervous feeling about what the future is going to bring." The driver said it made sense to prepare, even in a small way, for some kind of disaster.

LET'S STRIP

A driver picked a woman up outside a gentlemen's club. The woman got in the car; by the way she was dressed, the driver assumed she was a dancer. "Busy tonight?" the driver asked.

The woman said, "No. Couldn't get anyone to dance with me all night."

The driver responded, "That's a shame; you're a beautiful woman. You can dance for me, if you wish. I would love to see it." The next thing you know, the dancer started to play music on her phone and then proceeded to take her clothes off. The driver had to pull over because he couldn't drive and watch her dance at the same time. She had a perfect body: large breasts, tiny waist, and a tight, firm butt. Finally, all her clothes were off. There she was, lying totally nude in the back seat of the car.

The dancer told the driver that she had a condom if he had $100. The driver thanked her for the dance but didn't have $100. The dancer responded, "How much do you have?" The driver told the dancer he had no money and would have to take a rain check on the offer. By now the driver had offended the dancer. The dancer yelled at him to stop the car. The driver stopped, and the dancer jumped out of the car after putting her clothes on, calling him a faggot as she left.

COUNTRY SINGERS

A driver picked up four riders—two women and two men. They were all about twenty years old. They were going to a country concert with a big country star performing. They asked the driver if they could change the station to a country station. "Sure, go ahead," the driver responded.

Well, then the singing started. They knew every song that came on the radio. The harmonies and their voices were incredible. The group sang better than most artists we consider country stars today. It took about one hour to get to the concert, and the driver really enjoyed his personal concert on the way to the concert.

DAY OF SHOPPING

A driver picked a woman up. She wanted to go to the mall. Once they arrived at the mall, the woman asked the driver to wait. Thirty minutes had gone by, so the driver called the woman. She said, "I am on my way out."

The woman got back to the car and asked the driver to take her across the street to Best Buy. Again, she told the driver to wait; she would only be a couple of minutes. Another twenty minutes went by, and the woman finally came out. Once in the car, the woman told him to take her to the grocery store, which he did. The woman came out thirty minutes later with a cart full of food.

The driver helped her load all the groceries into the trunk and headed back to the woman's home. Once there, the woman asked the driver to help carry all the groceries into the house, which he did.

The total time the driver spent with this rider, including going to pick her up, was almost two hours. She gave him no tip because Uber said not to, and the total payment from Uber was eighteen dollars minus five dollars for gas, so the driver made thirteen dollars for himself. Uber has to raise the price. Once drivers smarten up and do the calculations, no one will keep driving for Uber.

DEATH OF FATHER

The diver picked up a rider who wanted to go to the main bus terminal. The driver noticed his eyes were red and bloodshot and had major dark circles, like he hadn't slept for a week. The rider started to bounce all over the back seat.

The rider told the driver that his father had just died. The driver said, "I am sorry to hear that."

The rider said, "It's okay; I never really knew him. But he left me three hundred thousand dollars in his will. It's a good thing, because I am unemployed."

The rider went on to tell the driver that he had told the funeral director to speed things up during the funeral. After the funeral, he had met with his father's lawyer. The lawyer had started to read the will, and the rider had said to the lawyer, "I don't give a fuck what it says; just give me the money."

The lawyer had said, "It's going to take a few weeks."

The rider had told the lawyer to go fuck himself. "I am here now, and I want my money."

The rider told the driver that he was hyper and had had to take four Xanax and smoke a joint just to meet with the lawyer. The driver asked the rider, "How did your father die?"

The rider said, "Who gives a fuck? I just want the money."

The driver said this guy kept talking nonstop, bouncing back and forth in the back seat. The driver was so happy when he pulled into the terminal and let this guy out. The driver thought to himself, How could anyone be so cold and callous?

A WOMAN'S FANTASY

A driver was telling me about a woman he picked up. She was very attractive, and they seemed to hit it off. The woman invited him up to her place for a drink. The driver said he had been driving most of the day and decided to go up for a drink. She poured them some Crown Royal. They sipped their whiskey and were just talking small talk when she moved over and sat right beside him.

They looked into each other's eyes and started to kiss, making out like teenagers. They took all their clothes off and went into the bedroom. The bedroom was dark, and he really couldn't see the room clearly, but they jumped in bed and started doing what couples do. She climbed on top of him and was driving him hard; it felt like she was going to drive right through the bed.

His eyes were finally adjusting to the room's light. The room came into focus. Then, out of the corner of his eye, he saw what looked like a man sitting in a chair, watching the whole thing go down. The driver jumped up, and the woman pushed him back on the bed and said, "It's my husband; he likes to watch."

Well, at that moment the driver said that he couldn't continue, but the woman wasn't giving up on their sexual encounter. The woman then climbed off and did everything sexually you could imagine to keep him in bed with her. The woman started giving him oral sex, while at the same time she attempted to force an object up his butt.

The driver couldn't believe what had just happened; he was in shock. He didn't know what to say to her or her husband. Finally he broke free, got dressed, and ran out the door.

SEX ANYWHERE

A driver picked up a couple. The driver noticed they were all over each other, kissing and touching. The driver turned around and said, "You guys just meet?"

They said, "Yes, two hours ago."

The driver said, "Great. It looks like you really enjoy each other's company."

As the driver was driving them to their destination, he looked in his rearview mirror and noticed the woman was sitting on the man's lap. Their breathing started getting heavy, and the woman was bouncing up and down like a yo-yo. The driver realized they were having sex in the back seat of his car, but there was nothing he could do at that moment. The driver arrived at their destination. The two of them straightened themselves and got out of his car. They never said a word to the driver and acted like nothing happened.

BETTER HIDE

A driver picked up a woman, and they both started sharing stories of their spouses and children. They got on the subject of sex. They talked about how they didn't find their spouses sexually attractive anymore and wanted to have a wild sexual encounter. The woman invited the driver back to her house.

They went in and went straight to the bedroom. She said no one was going to be home for hours. They started by taking each other's clothes off. Now they were both totally nude. They got into bed and started kissing passionately. They started to have intercourse. All of a sudden, they heard a door slam shut. They both jumped up. There was a man in the house calling for his wife.

The woman said to the driver, "You have to hide. He will kill both of us. He is really jealous." The driver panicked and hid under the bed.

The husband walked into the bedroom and said, "What you are doing home, in bed, with no clothes on?"

The wife turned around and said, "I didn't feel right, decided to come home and go to bed."

The husband then said, "With no clothes on? I haven't seen that in a long time." The husband started to take his clothes off and got into bed with his wife. The driver was under the bed while they both had sex.

Afterward the husband got up, said he had to get back to work and left. The driver climbed out from under the bed, got dressed, and told the woman, "I have to go," and left. The driver said he thought at any time he was going to be found out and shot.

LOST BY GPS

The GPS sending you to the wrong address happens more than anyone wants to admit to. I would say about 20 percent of the time, the GPS sends you to the wrong address. This is not a good situation. I have been sent to wrong addresses in a strange part of the city where there are almost no streetlights. The surroundings you may find yourself in are not the best. So you pull up to the house and call the rider, letting him or her know you have arrived. The rider says, "Well, where you are you? I don't see you." Then you repeat the address back to the rider. The address is wrong. If you're lucky, the rider will know where he or she is, but a lot of the time this is not the case.

This is especially true with tourists or people who maybe went downtown for a night out and are not familiar with their surroundings. The key with Uber—and what makes the company so successful (in theory)—is that you can be anywhere, you don't have to know where you are, and you can call an Uber. Usually the Uber follows the GPS on the riders' phones to find their locations.

I am not a techie person; I don't know why someone will be in one place, but the phone says he or she is somewhere else. It happens all the time. I can't tell you how many times I have driven through downtown city streets looking for riders. They depend on us to find them, and we can't let them down.

Another big problem with the GPS system is in construction zones. Many times I have been driving through a construction area, and my GPS says, "Turn right now," and I look, and there's a construction barrier. So I end up driving miles out of my way until I can find the rider. This is my biggest complaint with Uber other than the money.

BAD ONLINE DATE

A driver picked up a woman rider. She was young, about twenty-four years old. She wanted the driver to take her to a party that a guy she met online was having. The location was on the other side of the city.

The driver asked, "How long have you known this person?"

The woman said they had met online about three weeks ago, had talked a lot on the phone, and had met once for coffee.

The driver said the woman was so excited. It was going to be a costume party. The driver said, "That sounds like fun. What are you going as?"

The woman said, "I don't know." The guy she had met online was bringing her costume.

The driver thought to himself that this was strange, but who was he to judge? The driver started to ask questions like, "Do you know how many people are going to be there? Is it being held at a home or club? Do you know anybody else who is going?" The woman couldn't answer any of these questions.

As the driver pulled up to the location, he thought, "This doesn't look good." The streets were dark; it was not the best area of the city. He asked the woman, "Are you sure you want to go?" She said yes, so the driver let her out and watched as she went up to the location and knocked on the door. Someone opened the door, but there were no lights on in the house. The driver could not see who came to the door.

The driver told me he decided to hang for a while because he had a daughter around the same age, and this whole situation just didn't feel right to him. He could not leave in good conscience.

About a half hour later, as the driver was getting ready to leave, the front door opened up, and the woman came running out of the house screaming. The driver jumped out of the car and ran toward the girl. She was dressed in what looked like a white gown, and at first he didn't recognize her. A man was chasing her. They finally all collided. The man said to the driver that he was sorry, and they were just having a little fight. The man said, "She gets like this when she drinks too much." The man attempted to pull the woman back to the house. The driver turned to the man and said, "Look, I drove her here. I know the whole story, and she doesn't know you from Adam. I suggest you back off, or I am calling 911."

Finally, the driver got the woman into the car. She was still hysterical. The driver asked what had happened in the house. The woman said, "It was frightening—some people were dressed up as animals, and others were dressed in different types of robes. Everyone formed a circle and started chanting. In the center of the circle, there was an altar with all kinds of what looked like tools, with a picture of the devil at the center. I freaked out and ran." The driver's intuition saved the day this time.

BABYSITTER

This is a situation I find appalling. A driver picked up a woman and her two-year-old daughter. The woman told the driver she had an appointment. When they arrived at the destination, the woman said to the driver, "Will you watch my daughter? I will be just a couple of minutes." The woman went into the office, and there sat the driver, babysitting the little girl. The driver told me he was shocked; he would never leave his son or daughter with some driver he didn't know. To make matters worse, the woman was gone at least one half hour. How did that little girl feel, sitting there with a strange man?

The driver told me he had two girls and was able to keep the two-year-old occupied. The driver didn't want the little girl to start to cry because she missed her mother. The fact that the two-year-old wasn't upset with her mother being gone told the driver a lot about the mother. *What was the mother thinking?*

Once the mother returned to the car after her appointment, she asked the driver to take her to the Dunkin' Donuts drive-through. The total of her order was six dollars and eight cents. The rider then turned to the driver and asked him if he had eight cents. She did not want to break a one-dollar bill. The driver said he had seven cents, and the rider said, "That will do." When she went to pay the drive-through cashier, she told her she only had six dollars and seven cents and asked if that would be okay.

The cashier said, "Sure."

The driver thought, "What next from this woman?" Finally he drove them home. When she got out of the car, there was no tip, no "thank you for babysitting my daughter"—absolutely no response. The woman acted like it was normal for an Uber driver to babysit her daughter.

RADIO MANAGEMENT

This is one where the driver asked me if he could use names. I said, "Absolutely not." The driver told me this situation and the way these three guys (who were upper management in a large-market radio chain) talked was so over the top. These three guys talked about well-known radio personalities, calling them jerks, babies, and assholes. They talked about how if a radio personality didn't show up to do the scheduled event, they would make the personality's life a living hell and would get the engineer to mess up the personality's show. They went on to say, "Give him the wrong names of callers. Give him the wrong reason why they called. Interrupt with commercials when the radio personality doesn't expect them."

As an Uber driver, you will be present during a lot of situations like this one. The stories you will hear at times will be shocking—family battles, ugly divorces, and the list goes on. The driver learns just to drive without comment unless asked. You will find people will tell you all their personal history, like you were their therapist or priest. I guess to some drivers, this is what makes the job interesting and keeps the drivers working.

ORGY, ANYONE?

A driver picked up a woman. She wanted to be taken to this latest club. As the driver was driving her to the club, the woman started to tell the driver where she really wanted to go. The driver said, "Well, tell me where you really want to go." The rider told the driver that where she wanted to go only accepted couples, and she had no one to go with. The driver said, "I am stopping driving shortly. I will go with you."

The woman said, "Great; let's do it."

The rider directed the driver to a warehouse in the industrial area. They got out and walked up to a door. They knocked, and a bouncer type of person answered and said, "That will be a hundred dollars per person." The woman turned to the driver and said, "It's okay; I have it. You can buy the drinks."

The driver told me by this time he was feeling very anxious, not knowing what to expect. As they walked into the warehouse, he noticed a lot of different rooms—there were low lights and soft music playing, and people seemed to be making out everywhere he looked. Then he walked into the big room, and he couldn't believe his eyes. Couples were having sex everywhere. He watched as a man who was having sex with one woman got up and started to have sex with another one.

The driver was shocked, to say the least. He could not believe what he was witnessing—men and women having sex with multiple people. Threesomes were going on everywhere. The woman he'd come with had disappeared. Other women were coming up to him and pulling his clothes off.

I asked the driver, "So what you did you do?" You know the old saying, "When in Rome, do as the Romans do." The driver was French kissing one woman while at the same time, another woman was giving him oral sex. Then, without warning, some guy tried to fuck him up the butt, which he said he pushed aside. The driver told me by the time he left at about 4:00 a.m., he'd had sex with at least four different women and watched numerous people having sex with each other—just a totally insane night.

THROWN OUT OF CAR

A driver picked up four guys at a university. The driver could tell they had been drinking. They wanted to go to the professional football game that was in town. All of a sudden, as they were on the highway driving to the game, they all started to argue. The driver told them to calm down. Next thing you know, one of the guys in the back punched the guy in the front in the face.

The guy sitting in the front turned around in his seat and started punching into the back seat. Then all of them started to punch each other. The car was going all over the road with the back and forth of a full-blown fight.

The driver pulled over on the highway, jumped out, grabbed the first guy, and dragged him out of the car. Luckily the others in the back jumped out of the car to continue with the fight. The driver ran around, got back in the car, and took off, leaving them on the highway.

CLOTHING OPTIONAL

A driver picked up a woman and drove her to a nudist club. The driver asked the woman a lot of questions about the club and what went on there. Finally, the woman said to the driver, "Why don't you come over one night and check it out? You can leave your clothes on if you wish."

The driver decided to check it out. He arrived and walked in. It happened to be karaoke night. At first, he said, he left his clothes on. He looked around the room, and people were sitting at tables eating and drinking with no clothes on.

Have you ever sat at a bar while everyone around you was naked? It's a feeling that can't be explained. Then karaoke started. Watching these people sing and dance with no clothes on was a little much.

It was especially bad when the tempo of the music picked up, and everyone was shaking everything. It can't be explained in words—you had to be there.

The driver decided it wasn't for him and left.

RUN FOR YOUR LIFE

A driver arrived at the pickup spot to pick up a rider. The rider texted that she was in apartment 204. When she didn't come down, the driver went up to the apartment and knocked on the door. As he was standing there, a group of guys were walking down the hall toward him. One of them said, "That's him." They all started to run toward the driver. The driver, fearing for his life, decided to run. The driver ran out into the parking lot. He could hear them chasing him.

    The driver said he dove underneath a car. As he was hiding there, they walked around the car. He could see their feet, standing there, waiting for him to appear. The driver told me he was breathing so heavily that he was surprised they didn't hear him. For over an hour he hid under the car. Finally he crawled out, ran to his car, and took off.

NOT READY

A driver picked up a woman at a high-end mall. She got in the car and told the driver that she had canceled the other driver because he had been rude when she had tried to tell him where she was in the mall.

The woman started to tell the driver about her previous experience with Uber. She told the driver that the previous Uber driver had been so sexy that she had given him oral sex on the way to her destination. Then the driver had called a friend of his, and it had ended up becoming a threesome. The rider told the driver she loved threesomes.

As the driver was taking her to her destination, she would reach over and touch his crotch and say, "You're not ready yet." The driver felt under pressure to the advances of the rider but didn't really know what to do. The rider told the driver, "When you're hard enough, I will show you what young girls can't."

The driver asked the rider, "How old are you?"

"Forty-eight years old," she said, "and as tight and wet as a twenty-year-old."

The driver didn't know how to deal with this craziness. Again, she would reach over and grab his crotch. The driver just wanted it over. He thanked God when they arrived at her destination.

BAD CAR ODOR

A woman rider got in the car. As the driver was driving her to her destination, the rider commented on how she had had to contact Uber over the previous driver. The driver asked why. The rider said it was because his car stank so bad, you could barely breathe in the car. The driver asked, "What did it smell like?"

The rider said, "Old cigarettes and body odor. It was vile."

The previous driver had told this woman how he had to wait forty-five minutes for some people, and when they got into his car, all they did was complain that it smelled bad, and that was the thanks he got for waiting all that time. The rider had said to the driver, "It does smell really bad, like cigarettes." The driver had said he didn't smoke. The rider had said, "Then why is there a pack of cigarettes on your dash?"

The driver had said, "In case a rider wants one."

Then the driver had started to talk about how he wanted to quit.

The rider thought, "Definitely something is wrong with this driver."

Finally the driver had dropped her off at her destination. The woman had gone into the restaurant to meet her dinner guest, whom she had never met before. She had sat down for dinner with this person she had met online. They had shared pictures and phone conversation, but this had been their first face-to-face meeting.

Five minutes into the meeting, her date had looked down at his phone and said, "I have a bit of an emergency that I have to take care of now. Can we reschedule?"

The woman had said, "Sure," and the man had gotten up and left the restaurant.

The woman swore it was because of the odor coming off her clothes after riding in that Uber driver's car. The present driver asked, "Have you been able to reschedule the dinner?"

The woman said, "No, it's not going to happen."

GUNS

A driver arrived in a bad part of town to pick up a rider. When he pulled into the complex, he noticed four or five guys hanging around with guns on them. The driver called the rider and told her about the situation. She said for the driver to come anyway—she would have them put their guns away.

The driver sat there for a moment, thinking, "There is no way I am going near those guys." Then, all of a sudden, police cars came racing into the complex. The police jumped out of their cars, and then the driver heard gunfire.

The driver told me he raced out of that complex, knowing the police were there, putting their lives on the line to deal with the gun-toting group.

SENIOR ENCOUNTER

On numerous occasions, a driver had to pick up this woman who appeared to be maybe eighty years old. This woman looked in great shape for her age, dressed well, and always had perfect makeup. The driver said they would talk about everything. The woman walked two miles a day to keep herself in shape.

One day he picked her up as usual. Their conversation turned to her relationship with her husband, who'd passed away over twenty years ago. The woman, out of the blue, brought up sex—the fact that she hadn't had sex in over twenty-five years and yearned for it every day. She asked the driver if he thought that was normal for a woman her age to have these strong feelings. The driver said, "Of course it is. You're human, and age should have nothing to do with your desires." The woman went on to say how she wanted, more than anything else, to have sex at least one more time before she passed on.

Next, the woman told the driver how much she enjoyed his company and how she found him extremely attractive, and she asked whether she could have his permission to touch his body. The driver didn't know what to say. The woman again said, "Please let me touch your body. I promise I won't hurt you," with a smile and glint in her eye.

The driver finally said, "Okay." The driver described how she gently massaged his thigh and crotch area. As the driver pulled up to her home, the woman asked him to come in for a cup of coffee or glass of wine. The driver found himself caught up in the situation and decided to go in for a few minutes. Once inside, the woman poured him and herself a glass of wine. They sat there and talked about everything. Again, sex was brought up. The woman went over to the driver and started to touch his crotch area and suggested they go into her bedroom. The driver told her he really had to go, but the woman wouldn't take no for an answer. She unzipped his fly and started to perform oral sex on him. The driver could not believe the situation he found himself in. He told me he remembered looking down at this eighty-year-old woman as she performed oral sex on him and thought, "What the fuck am I doing?" Then she got up, sat on his lap, and rode him. When it was over, the woman thanked him and told him she would never forget that day. He had made one of her items on her bucket list come true.

JEALOUS BOYFRIEND

A driver picked up a couple. When the couple entered the car, the woman glanced over at the driver and smiled. As they were driving to the couple's destination, the woman kept looking at the driver and smiling. The driver felt a little uncomfortable with these looks. He could tell the man was upset over the whole situation. Then, all of a sudden, the man yelled at the driver, "Who the fuck are you looking at? Keep your eyes on the road, and don't let me see you staring at my girlfriend again. Do you do this with all the women that get in your car? Asshole."

The driver didn't want to escalate the situation, so he kept quiet and dared not look into his rearview mirror.

The man started into his girlfriend: "Why would you look at an asshole cab driver like that? What the fuck is wrong with you?" The tension in the car was so thick you could have cut it with a knife.

Then the woman turned around and said to him, "That's what you get for fucking Ashley. Two can play the same game." She told him he was nothing but a disgusting pig and that it was over between them. She never wanted to see him again.

The driver was thinking, "What could possibly happen next?" Just when he thought it couldn't get any worse, it did—she slapped the man in the face. He started calling her a bitch from hell and said that she was useless in bed, and that was why he had to get it elsewhere.

The driver stepped in and said, "If you both don't stop, you can get out now, and I will call 911." They both shut up, and the rest of the ride seemed to last forever. Finally, they arrived at their destination. He thanked God they were gone.

FEMALE DRIVERS

There are a lot of young female drivers coming on board. This is due to Uber targeting the eighteen- to twenty-two-year-olds for drivers. In my opinion, when they dropped the drivers' rate per mile from $1.30 to $0.95 (and they have dropped it again), they lost a lot of professional drivers who chose to drive for Uber for their career. But one-third of their income was taken away. This made driving for Uber not viable as a career choice.

Uber is targeting this group because for a lot of them, their options are to work in retail or the food industry for minimum wage or to drive for Uber at minimum wage. Most of this group may not calculate all the costs related to driving for Uber and may feel it's a better choice than working retail.

I haven't come across a lot of female drivers, but those I have spoken to seem to send the same message: Don't drive at night—this is when the bars and clubs empty out. People are intoxicated and will do and say things, especially to young female drivers, that they normally would not do or say if they were sober.

As a driver, you come across mature situations that a young person may not be equipped to handle. For example, a young female driver told me she once picked up three guys. They got into her car, and she could tell they were drunk. One of them started to make passes at her, telling her she was beautiful and had a great body, and he asked if her breasts were real. The other male passenger suggested they should all feel her breasts, and between the three of them, they should be able to tell if they were real or not. The driver told me she started to freak out, not knowing how far these three drunk guys would go.

Luckily there was an accident up the road, and police were everywhere. The guys' minds were taken off her and onto the accident. It seemed after they drove by the crash, the guys quieted down and never said much at all after that.

The female driver still wonders what may have happened if it wasn't for the accident.

Another problem is that some female drivers bring along a passenger for safety reasons. I have had some riders complain to me about this situation. Many times there are four people that call for the Uber, and when it arrives, they can't all get in the car, so they have to call for another Uber—very unhappy riders.

GENTLEMEN'S CLUB

Other Uber drivers and I are amazed by how many people (both male and female) we drive to gentlemen's clubs. The females usually accompany their husbands or boyfriends that go to the gentlemen's clubs, surprisingly wanting their husbands or boyfriends to watch the girls dance. A lot of the time, the wife or girlfriend wants to watch as the boyfriend or husband receives sexual favors from these girls. Many drivers have driven couples who were taking dancers home.

We know why the men go. Sometimes we will pick guys up at the airport and drive them directly to the gentlemen's club. The stories that the guys talk about when we pick them up from the gentlemen's club are something you would only read about in *Penthouse* or *Playboy*.

I have found most of the men that frequent these clubs are married. When the men are asked, "Why do you go to these clubs?" the main reason is that their wives aren't interested sexually in them anymore. Most guys can't remember the last time their wives gave them oral sex. During the beginning of their marriage, oral sex was almost daily. Even if their wives weren't up to having sex, their wives would always do something else sexually with them. The one thing I know for sure is that if women don't want their men going to places like these gentlemen's clubs, they should try not to say no. It's a fact that if a man is turned down more than three times, he will give up trying and start to look elsewhere.

POOL PARTY

A driver picked up a twentysomething girl. The girl sat right beside him wearing the skimpiest bikini that he had ever seen with no cover-up. The driver reported, "She was busting out of the suit." So on the way to the pool party, they struck up some great conversation. As he went to drop her off at the pool party, she turned to the driver and suggested maybe he should also come to the party. The driver thanked her for the offer but said he had to work.

One hour later he received a call for a pickup at the same place he had dropped this woman off. When the rider came out, it was the same woman he had just dropped off. The driver said, "What happened?" She said the people there were boring.

But the woman said she was having a pool party at her house and asked the driver to come. The driver told her he didn't have a bathing suit. She said, "Don't worry about it. I will find you one." The driver told her to call him later if she still wanted him to come.

Two hours later, he received a phone call from this woman, again inviting him to her pool party. The driver agreed to go. The driver told me he didn't know why she wanted him to come; he was in his early fifties, and she was in her twenties.

The driver arrived at the party. There were about twenty people there, all in their twenties. He felt out of place and was going to leave when this woman came up to him, grabbed his hand, and said, "You're not going anywhere. You're with me tonight." The driver and the woman started to have a few drinks. By this time it was getting late. A lot of the people had left. So the driver and woman got into the pool. They hugged and held each other, just moving around the pool. She then proceeded to remove her bathing suit. Now she was totally nude.

The driver was shocked when she slipped her hand down his bathing suit and asked him to sit on the edge of the pool. Before he knew it, she had his bathing suit off and had started giving him oral sex on the edge of the pool. Within minutes he jumped into the pool, where they had sex. The driver couldn't believe it; there he was having sex in a pool with a beautiful young woman.

The driver told me this was the first and last time they got together.

DUMPSTER DIVING

A driver was called to a plaza to pick up a rider. The driver ended up going to the back of the plaza to find his riders. When he arrived, the two guys he was picking up had a lot of items to load into his trunk. The guys loaded the items into the trunk and got in the car. The driver asked, "What's with all the stuff in the trunk?" The guys went on to tell him that they went into Dumpsters to look for items to resell. The driver said, "Really?" The two guys went on to tell him that was what they did for money to fund their college education. The driver turned around and asked, "Do you mean to tell me you make enough money off of Dumpster diving to pay for all your bills?"

They said, "Absolutely. The other day we found a juicer still in the box that we sold for eighty dollars. We found a pair of expensive boots, and we sold them for forty dollars. We found a jewelry box full of cosmetics and some gold jewelry."

The driver thought, "Wow, free enterprise at its finest."

GLAZED DOUGHNUT

I picked up this Uber driver and asked him, as I do with every Uber driver, "Tell me about a passenger who sent you over the edge with his or her actions."

The driver went on to tell me about this woman he picked up: "She sat in the front seat beside me. This woman was very aggressive and asked me a lot of sexual questions." The driver had tried to pass it off and make a joke about the situation. "We really hit it off. Then she asked me if I liked oral sex." The driver had said, "Sure."

She had said, "Giving or receiving?"

The driver had said, "Both."

He continued, "Then we both climbed into the back seat. She slowly pulled down my pants and started to give me oral sex right away. Then I started to give her oral sex at the same time." The driver couldn't believe what they were doing right in the open.

Then, suddenly she started to scream. "I am cumming"

"Suddenly she exploded all over my head, covering my whole head with her cum. There was so much cum that it got into my mouth, which caused me to throw up right away. There I was with my head covered with cum, which felt like a creamed doughnut, and at the same time I was throwing up in my car.

"Needless to say, I had a major mess in my car. I couldn't drive for Uber for days until I had my car professionally cleaned." The driver told me he didn't think he would ever be able to give a woman oral sex again.

THE FLOATER

A driver told me about a woman he had picked up. She wanted to go to the beach and watch the sunset. She asked him if it was okay. "Sure," he said. The driver didn't care, as he was being paid anyway. They arrived at the beach, and the woman got out and asked the driver to walk with her along the water's edge. As they were walking and talking, the woman asked the driver how adventurous he was. The driver said, "Very."

Then she turned to him and said, "Let's go skinny-dipping."

The driver told me he didn't know why, but off came the clothes, and into the water they went. While in the water, the driver had to go to the bathroom really badly. He couldn't hold it, so he decided to move a little away from the woman and go in the water. Well, the driver said the crap floated to the surface. As he tried to move away from the crap, it kept following him. Now the woman was calling him over. The faster he moved toward the woman, the faster the crap came after him. There he was, just a few feet away from the woman, and this floating crap was a few feet behind him. Finally he grabbed her hand and told her to run to shore because he thought he'd seen a shark. It was the only way to get away from the floating crap. After they got to shore, she pushed him down in the sand, jumped on him, and rode him like he was a wild horse as the waves were washing up against them.

The whole time the wild sex was happening, he was in fear that the crap would float up onto shore and somehow get caught up between them. The driver was so relieved when it was over and the crap had not reached shore.

LAST SEX WISH

A driver told me a sad story about a woman he picked up. She got into the car with a full-length coat on. It wasn't cold out, and the driver thought it was kind of odd to be wearing this long coat. She then asked the driver to drive her to a nearby park. When they arrived at the park, the woman started to tell the driver that she was terminally ill, and one thing on her bucket list was to have sex with a perfect stranger. She told the driver, "You can't catch cancer." As the driver turned around to say something, the woman opened her coat, exposing her totally naked body to the driver. The woman added, "If we decide to have sex, it will be only once. We will never, ever have contact again. Is that understood?"

The driver was in a major dilemma—should he grant this woman her dying wish or wish her luck and hope she found someone else to complete her bucket list?

The driver looked at her naked body again. The woman was beautiful—she had a great body. "Oh, what the hell; let's go for it," he thought. He climbed onto the back seat and started to play with her breasts. She unzipped his pants and started to play with his penis. The driver climbed on top and gently entered her. He felt unsure, because of her illness, how hard to push. But to his surprise, she screamed out, "Harder, harder." The driver drove her hard, driving her so hard that he thought that he would push her right through the back seat of the car. When it was over, she closed her coat and coldly said, "Please drive me home." Not one word was said on the way back. She got out of the car, and he was never to see her again.

WORKING-GIRL CHAUFFEUR

A driver picked up a woman at a hotel. She was black and beautiful. Her lips were full, and she had large eyes. Her clothes were very revealing, leaving little to the imagination. Needless to say, she was a perfect ten. The woman told the driver she had a lot of places to go and asked if he was up to spending a few hours with her. The driver responded, "No problem." The woman let him know she would take good care of him. Off they went from expensive hotel to expensive hotel. The driver initially didn't have a clue what was going on. She would spend about a half hour at each hotel. The driver heard her on her phone making arrangements with someone about where to go next. After about four hours of his driving her around, the woman asked him to take her home. When they arrived at her house, the woman gave the driver a fifty-dollar tip and asked him if he would like a sexual favor of his choice.

The driver told me she was so beautiful that he couldn't say no. He wanted oral sex. The woman then had him open the car door and stand up with his body facing into the car. She unzipped his pants, gently reached in, and took out his penis. There was the driver standing up on the sidewalk where everyone could see, getting a blow job from this beautiful woman. Afterward, they parted ways, and the driver never saw her again.

WHO ARE UBER DRIVERS?

I have met a lot of Uber drivers. I am truly amazed by the diverse backgrounds of these drivers. I will mention a few here:

A medical doctor: I asked him why he would ever want to drive for Uber. He told me being a doctor was not a license to print money; with all his overhead costs, it was hard to make ends meet.

A business broker: "The way business sales are, I have to work two jobs."

An author: "It helps with my creative side—meeting so many different people who all have great stories."

A dancer/stripper: "With today's economics, tips aren't what they used to be. I need the extra money. I am used to working with different people, so it's a natural for me."

An investment banker: "Most people don't realize the true nature of the economy. It's in total shambles. Over the last seven years, the amount of debt we have incurred cannot be repaid. I am trying to make extra money for when it all collapses."

A bartender: "Have you seen the price of meat lately, especially bacon? You need three jobs to survive."

I could go on forever with all the unique drivers I have met. But from these few mentioned here, you can see everyone has a story and a reason to drive. So does everyone you pick up as a rider, making for one interesting moment in time for all involved.

To be an Uber driver, I feel you must be great with people and be able to carry on conversation with anyone on a variety of subjects, Also, you must be comfortable with the fact that you never know where you may be going or—the bigger issue, maybe—who you will be picking up and allowing to ride with you in your vehicle.

FINAL NOTE ON MONEY AND UBER

One more comment about the money: As I am writing this part of the book, Uber is texting me. It's a holiday long weekend. Uber says, "Make up to $23.00 per hour working from 10:00 p.m. to 4:00 a.m." Well, you know what that means if you're a driver, but let's take up to $23 per hour and break it down to reality. Uber takes the first dollar. $23 - $1= $22.

Then Uber takes 20 percent of the $22, which equals $4.40. We subtract the $4.40 from the $22 and get $15.60, which is left for the driver.

Now we have the driver expenses: gas at $2.50 per hour plus depreciation and wear and tear on the car at minimum $1.25 per hour. The driver's minimum cost for their car is $3.75 per hour. Let's subtract the $3.75 per hour from the $15.60, or your share of the $23. This leaves you with $11.85 an hour. The fact Uber is advertising this tells you they must have lost any concept of the true expenses of owning a vehicle.

PRESS RELEASE

A *Newswire* article from April 27, 2012, reads, "AAA released the results of its annual Your Driving Costs' study today revealing a 1.9% rise in the yearly costs to own and operate a sedan in the U.S. The average cost per mile is 59.6 cents per mile, or $8,946 per year, based upon 15,000 miles of annual driving."

You can look up the study and read all the details, but think about this for a moment: Uber pays their drivers $0.95 per mile. The cost is almost $0.60 per mile. The driver nets $0.35 per Uber-driven mile. This does not count the miles on the way to the pickup or to return to your area after the drop-off, which can double the actual mileage driven by the driver.

So the driver's real costs may be well over $1 per mile. Drivers, you are possibly working for free or next to it.

Drivers have to unite and force Uber to pay a minimum of $1.30 per mile, which is what they used to pay. If not, it's a free country. Work for free—it's your choice.

Have you ever wondered why most Uber drivers don't know any other Uber drivers? It's a smart move by corporate—divide and conquer.

Imagine for a moment we all got together and went through the actual costs to be a driver. Then we demanded a reasonable return for our efforts. What happens to the Uber model then? I think it's all *over*!

Update: Uber has again dropped their payments another 20 percent, down to about $0.65 per mile. That means drivers end up with a true profit of about $0.06 per mile.

Wake up, Uber drivers of America!

New Update: Uber has increased their payments to $0.80 per mile.

One Final Word about Uber and Its Drivers

I would estimate about 30 percent of Uber drivers should not be driving for Uber.

Here are my reasons why:

First, so many female riders have told me that either the Uber driver would ask them out or constantly compliment them. They felt uncomfortable with the Uber driver's advances, but as I have said earlier, most women were afraid to report the drivers to Uber out of fear. They would tell me the Uber driver knew where they lived.

Second, Uber has to be losing millions in sales due to the fact that a lot of these drivers have told the passengers to call them directly the next time they needed a ride and thus eliminate Uber. In turn, the customer would save money.

I must say, when I was driving for Uber, I was approached by numerous riders asking me for my number to call me directly. So it's not just the drivers who are asking to call them directly—it's also the riders.

This is a situation Uber is going to have to deal with without making false accusations against all drivers, as they have done in the past.

I personally had Uber e-mail me, suggesting that I was taking on riders for cash and eliminating Uber. I wrote Uber back and told them to show me one person that had made such an accusation. They couldn't because I never took cash from any riders. This is the type of blanket threats they must be sending out to everyone, hoping to put the fear of God into the drivers.

Uber, pay your drivers at least $1.30 a mile. You will get a better class of professional driver, as you had initially, before you reduced the drivers' rate to where quality drivers had to leave. Now the type of driver Uber is attracting has to ask this one question: Should I work for Uber or for McDonald's?

The truth is you will end up making more money working for McDonald's.

ABOUT THE AUTHOR

Douglas has written other published works that you may find interesting.
 Christians Remember Your Past lives-Learn How
 Live Your Life in AWE!

Contact Information
Douglas Casimiri
1324 Seven Springs Blvd. #145
New Port Richey, FL 34655
This is a great book detailing what's involved in being an Uber driver, the kind of income you could expect, and some situations you may find yourself in as a driver.

www.ingramcontent.com/pod-product-compliance
Lightning Source LLC
Chambersburg PA
CBHW071443180526
45170CB00001B/442